AMERICAN PRESIDENTS

Barack Obama

by Rebecca Pettiford

BELLWETHER MEDIA • MINNEAPOLIS, MN

BLASTOFF!
READERS
2

Blastoff! Readers are carefully developed by literacy experts to build reading stamina and move students toward fluency by combining standards-based content with developmentally appropriate text.

 Level 1 provides the most support through repetition of high-frequency words, light text, predictable sentence patterns, and strong visual support.

 Level 2 offers early readers a bit more challenge through varied sentences, increased text load, and text-supportive special features.

 **Level 3** advances early-fluent readers toward fluency through increased text load, less reliance on photos, advancing concepts, longer sentences, and more complex special features.

★ **Blastoff! Universe**

Reading Level

Grade **K**

Grades **1–3**

Grade **4**

This edition first published in 2022 by Bellwether Media, Inc.

No part of this publication may be reproduced in whole or in part without written permission of the publisher. For information regarding permission, write to Bellwether Media, Inc., Attention: Permissions Department, 6012 Blue Circle Drive, Minnetonka, MN 55343.

Library of Congress Cataloging-in-Publication Data

Names: Pettiford, Rebecca, author.
Title: Barack Obama / by Rebecca Pettiford.
Description: Minneapolis, MN : Bellwether Media, 2022. | Series: American presidents | Includes bibliographical references and index. | Audience: Ages 5-8 | Audience: Grades 2-3 | Summary: "Relevant images match informative text in this introduction to Barack Obama. Intended for students in kindergarten through third grade"--Provided by publisher.
Identifiers: LCCN 2021011379 (print) | LCCN 2021011380 (ebook) | ISBN 9781644875117 (library binding) | ISBN 9781648344794 (paperback) | ISBN 9781648344190 (ebook)
Subjects: LCSH: Obama, Barack--Juvenile literature. | Presidents--United States--Biography--Juvenile literature. | African American politicians--Biography--Juvenile literature. | Politicians--United States--Biography--Juvenile literature.
Classification: LCC E908 .P48 2022 (print) | LCC E908 (ebook) | DDC 973.932092 [B]--dc23
LC record available at https://lccn.loc.gov/2021011379
LC ebook record available at https://lccn.loc.gov/2021011380

Editor: Elizabeth Neuenfeldt   Designer: Josh Brink

Printed in the United States of America, North Mankato, MN.

Table of Contents

Who Is Barack Obama?

Barack Obama was the 44th
president of the United States.
He was the first Black president.

Barack served from 2009 to 2017.

Barack's Hometown

N
W E
S

Honolulu,
Hawaii

Barack was born
in Hawaii in 1961.
He moved to Indonesia
when he was six.

He went to school there until fifth grade. Then, he finished school in Hawaii.

Barack studied at Columbia **University**. Then, he became a **community organizer**. He liked working with people.

Presidential Picks

Food

chili

Hobbies

collecting comic books and reading

Sport

basketball

Music

Stevie Wonder

8

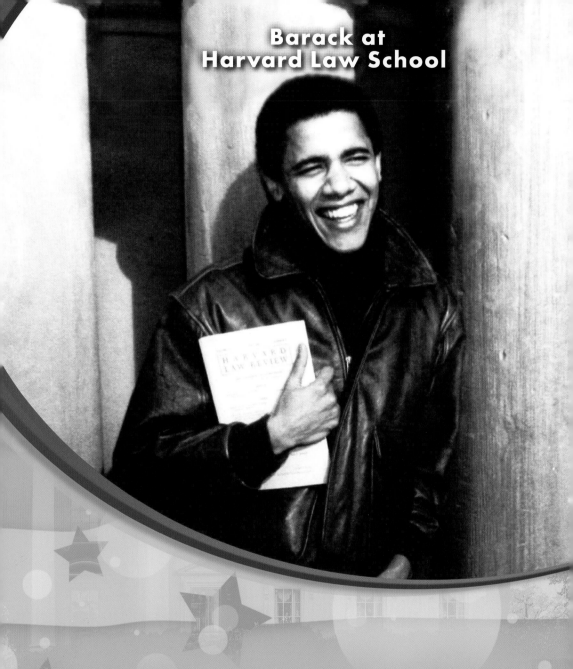

Later, he studied at Harvard Law
School. He became a **lawyer**.

Barack was an Illinois state **senator** in 1997. He worked to help children and poor people.

Barack wanted to help more people. He became a U.S. senator in 2005.

What helped Barack
become president?

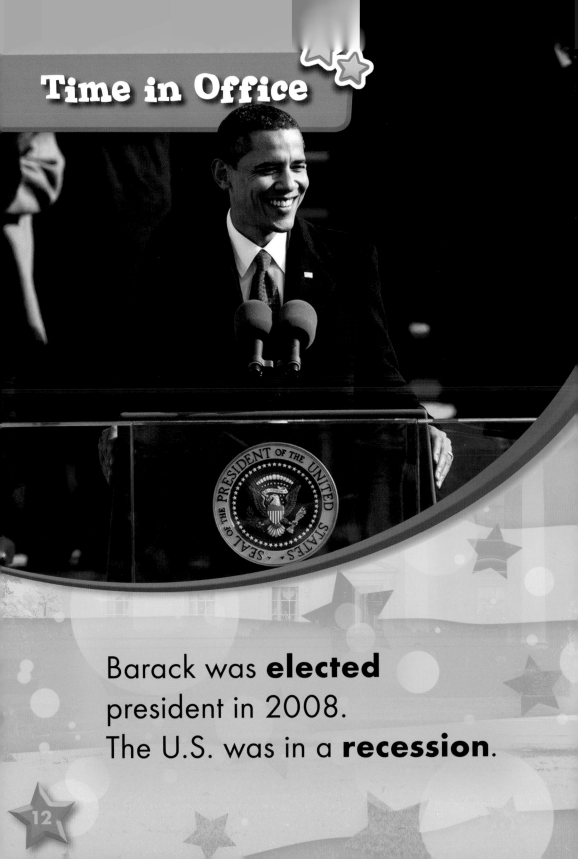

Barack was **elected** president in 2008. The U.S. was in a **recession**.

Barack made the **economy** stronger. More people could work again!

Presidential Profile

Place of Birth

Honolulu, Hawaii

Birthday

August 4, 1961

Schooling

Columbia University and Harvard Law School

Term

2009 to 2017

Party

Democratic

Signature

Vice President

Joe Biden

In 2010, Barack signed the **Affordable Care Act**.

Barack signing the Affordable Care Act

Some people thought it would not work. But it helped millions of people get health care!

Barack also helped end the **Iraq War**. He brought many U.S. troops home.

The war ended in 2011.

Barack announcing the Iraq War is over

16

Barack welcoming
U.S. troops

17

Barack with world leaders

Barack was reelected in 2012. He worked to slow **climate change**. He made plans to use clean **energy**. He worked with leaders around the world.

Barack Timeline

November 4, 2008

Barack Obama is elected president

March 23, 2010

Barack signs the Patient Protection and Affordable Care Act

December 15, 2011

The Iraq War ends

November 6, 2012

Barack is reelected

August 3, 2015

Barack introduces the Clean Power Plan

January 20, 2017

Barack leaves office

What Barack Left Behind

Barack left office in 2017. As the first Black president, he **inspired** many people.

He also helped people get
the health care they needed!

Glossary

Affordable Care Act—a law passed in 2010 that was made to provide affordable health insurance to all Americans through the government; the Affordable Care Act is also called Obamacare.

climate change—a human-caused change in Earth's weather due to warming temperatures

community organizer—someone who brings people together for a purpose

economy—the way a state or country makes, sells, and uses goods and services

elected—chosen by voting

energy—power that comes from heat, water, or electricity

inspired—gave someone an idea about what to do or create

Iraq War—a U.S.-led war fought between Iraq and many other countries that happened from 2003 to 2011

lawyer—a person trained to help people with matters relating to the law

recession—a period of time in which many people do not have jobs

senator—a member of the Senate of the U.S. government; the Senate helps make laws.

university—a school that people go to after high school

To Learn More

AT THE LIBRARY

Benjamin, Jenny. *Barack Obama*. North Mankato, Minn.: Capstone Press, 2019.

Jenner, Caryn. *What Is an Election?* New York, N.Y.: DK Publishing, 2020.

Stoltman, Joan. *Barack Obama*. New York, N.Y.: Gareth Stevens Publishing, 2018.

ON THE WEB

FACTSURFER

Factsurfer.com gives you a safe, fun way to find more information.

1. Go to www.factsurfer.com.

2. Enter "Barack Obama" into the search box and click 🔍.

3. Select your book cover to see a list of related content.

Index